To........

D1101157

From....................

Purple Ronnie's

Little Book for a

Lovely Grandma

by Purple Ronnie

First published 2008 by Boxtree
an imprint of Pan Macmillan Ltd
Pan Macmillan, 20 New Wharf Road, London N1 9RR
Basingstoke and Oxford
Associated companies throughout the world
www.panmacmillan.com

ISBN 978-0-7522-2641-5

A CIP catalogue record for this book is
available from the British Library.

much
better

a poem for a

Special Grandma

You're a really special Grandma
And you mean a lot to me
When you're around
You make the world
A better place to be!

Special Tip

Grandmas REALLY know how to spoil you

so it's fizzy drinks and chocolates for breakfast in my house!
pop
yippee! hooray!
bye kids
fume
gritted teeth

Granny Pants

Grandmas wear knickers that look like a whole outfit on their own

Grandchildren

Grandmas NEVER stop boasting about how amazing their grandchildren are

Look! Her very first wee wee on the potty. Isn't she clever!
v. bored

Rules of Being a Grandma - Nº 1

In order to show that you've still got all your own hair you must dye it a very peculiar colour

a poem about

Grandmas

Some grandmas can be batty
And can drive you round the
bend
But you're not just a
brilliant one
You're also a fab friend !

Drinking

All grandmas love
to have a little tipple
at lunchtime

Frills

Grandmas like to make EVERYTHING frilly

Special Tip

Sometimes it's easier
to talk to your grandma
than it is to your mum

Driving

Warning:- Some grandmas can be a bit of a hazard in the car

Rules of Being a Grandma - Nº 2

Whenever you take your specs off, you must ALWAYS forget where you left them

a poem about

Granny Boobs

You know you're another year
older
When the bits that the men
used to squeeze
Aren't bobbing around by your
chest anymore
...They're dangling down by your
knees!

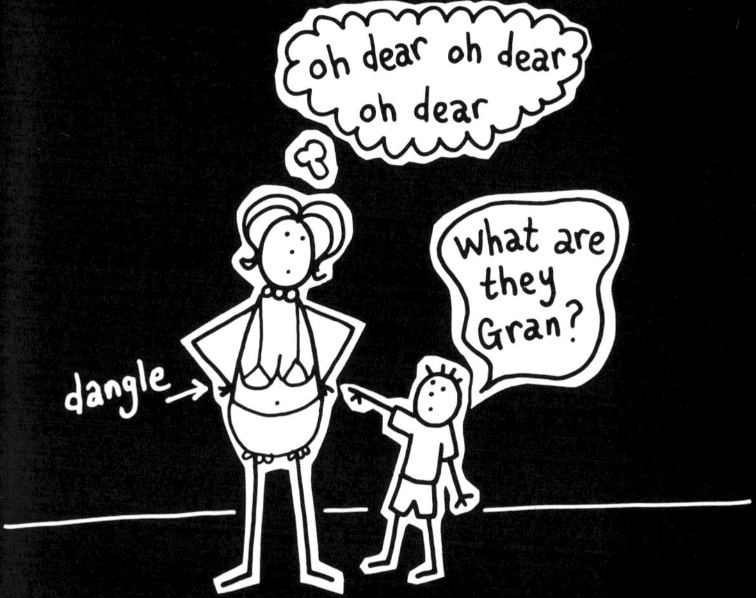
oh dear oh dear oh dear
What are they Gran?
dangle

Fashion

Grandmas are not ALWAYS in touch with the latest trends

Warning

Grandmas love to give you big sloppy wet kisses. Watch out for the prickly hairs on their chins

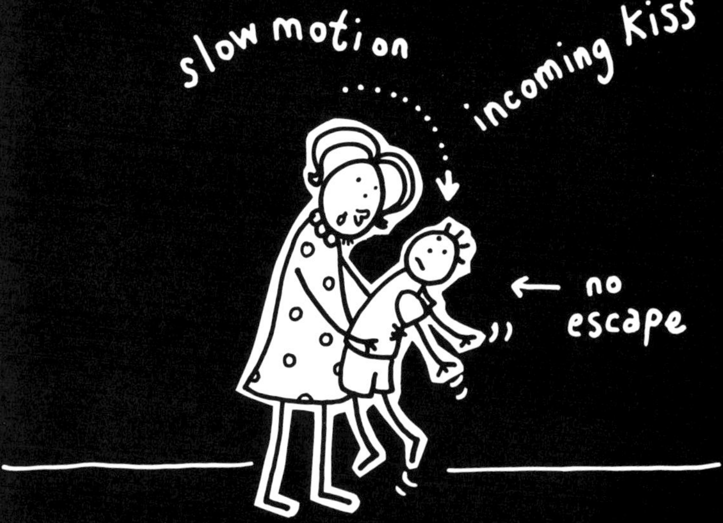
slow motion
incoming kiss
no escape

Age

Grandmas never have to say EXACTLY how old they are

Technology

Grandmas get very over-excited when they find out how to work new technology

Rules of Being a Grandma Nº 3

Grandma's cupboards must ALWAYS smell of lavender

a poem for a

Fab Grandma

Being a grandma's a
difficult job
That's not always easy to do
But if I could choose
The best grandma around
I know I would go and pick
you!

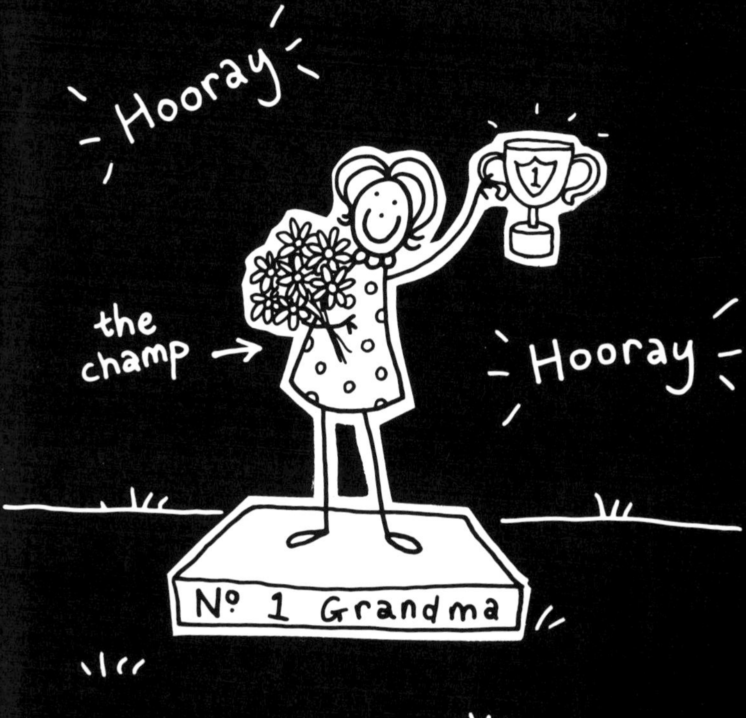
Hooray
the champ
Hooray
1
Nº 1 Grandma

Pets

Grandmas can sometimes pay TOO much attention to their pets

Cooking

No-one knows how to
do home cooking quite
like your grandma does

You don't deserve her, you lazy, good-for-nothing scallywag...!
Sherry

Soaps

Grandmas can get very involved with their favourite soaps on TV

Warning

Sometimes grandmas don't have complete control of their bodies

And I saw old Bert looking over the hedge and do you know what he said...?
not this one again!

Rules of Being a Grandma - N° 4

All grandmas LOVE talking to their plants

a poem for a

Top Grandma

This short little poem
Is specially to say
You're a really top
                grandma
You're lovely! Wahey!

who wants biscuits?
and strawberries!
and ice-cream!
amazing
me!
me!

Tablets

No matter what's wrong with them, grandmas always have a tablet for everything

Honesty

Grandmas sometimes find it hard to keep their thoughts to themselves

he's got rather straggly hair hasn't he, and what's that silly beard for?
gran!
tug
new boyfriend

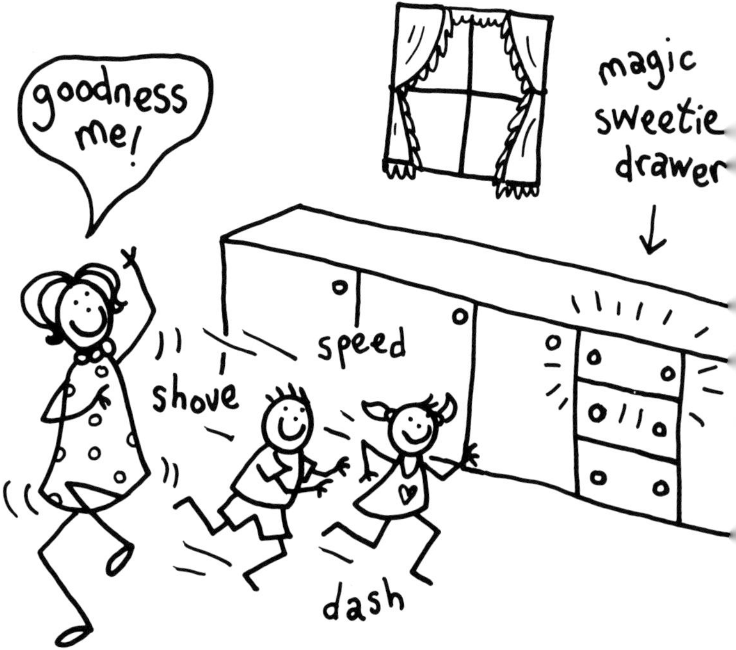
goodness me!
magic sweetie drawer
speed
shove
dash

Special Tip

Grandmas always have a secret drawer LOADED with treats

Hairdressing

Grandmas love to spend ages at the hairdresser under special granny machines

wheeee!
lovely kip
ZZZZ
leap
help me!
come on Scottie!
slide
give it back!
No!
chase

Rules of Being a Grandma - N° 5

There's nothing a grandma loves more than a good afternoon nap

a poem for a

Wonderful Grandma

I know that it sounds
cheesy
But it happens to be true
There couldn't be another
grandma
Quite as cool as you!

Sweet Dreams